A Special Gift

To _____

From _____

Before I Give You Away

Before I Give You Away

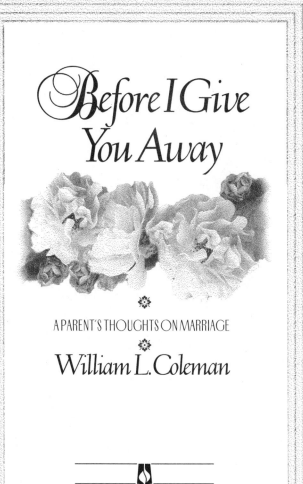

❖

A PARENT'S THOUGHTS ON MARRIAGE

❖

William L. Coleman

BETHANY HOUSE PUBLISHERS
Minneapolis, Minnesota 55438

Published by Bethany House Publishers
A Ministry of Bethany Fellowship, Inc.
11300 Hampshire Avenue South
Minneapolis, Minnesota 55438

Printed in the United States of America.

**Library of Congress
Cataloging-in-Publication Data**

Coleman, William L.
    Before I give you away / William L. Coleman.
        p.   cm.

    1. Marriage—Religious aspects—Christianity.
2. Fathers and daughters. I. Title.
BV4012.27.C65   1994
248.4—dc20   94–47145
ISBN 1–55661–487–X   CIP

To Phil and June

WILLIAM L. COLEMAN is the well-known author of over thirty Bethany House books on a variety of topics. Combining his experience as a pastor, researcher, writer, and speaker, he is noted for his effective communication in the area of family relationships and practical spirituality. He has been married for over thirty years and is the father of three children.

Contents

❖

We Aren't Envious!

*S*ome of the greatest satisfaction you will ever receive in this life will come from your marriage. Hiking, biking, and water slide rides might be fun, but let's get real. They don't hold a candle to close encounters with the person you love.

June and Phil, we aren't jealous. We still enjoy our own marriage too much to ever get jealous over someone else's. But we do ask that God will give you loving hearts, thoughtful spirits, and a small, chilly bedroom so you have to snuggle a lot.

Good Choice!

ongratulations or best wishes or whatever it is we're supposed to say. No matter—there aren't words strong enough or warm enough to say how happy we are for you.

Your mom and I like your choice in men. I especially like the way you look at each other. The way the light dances in your eyes when you're together, the playful grin on your lips, the way you beam when he walks into the room. You don't have the look of anxiety or the tension that goes with un-certainty. The two of you look comfortable together. More than comfortable. You're

like happy magnets that spin out and then
hurry toward each other whenever you get
close.

You were always too smart to "grab a
guy." I never felt your goal was to just get
married. You centered on a person and not
your situation. Even though you made a
quick decision, you based your choice on a
deep and genuine love for a terrific person.
When you know, you know.

Allow yourself the luxury of being tre-
mendously proud of your future husband.
Never shrink back and be bashful about
your total satisfaction. Too many spouses
hem and haw and half apologize over the
person they marry. It's a false and shallow
humility.

Always feel as proud as you are today
that God allowed such a wonderful person
to come into your life. Not because he is in-
telligent or good-looking or a Christian,
though he is all of that. Be thankful that he
is such a good, caring, and thoughtful person. If every good and perfect gift comes
from God, it looks like you got a package
straight through the celestial express.

You're probably thinking that if we didn't like Phil, we wouldn't tell you anyway. And you're right. I'd make up something goofy about him wearing nice ties or being a good Ping-Pong player. But you made it easy. You brought home a great guy and we love being around him.

Life affords us only so many genuine pleasures, and being married to a person you cherish, love, and enjoy rates right up there as the most pleasurable of all.

Feel satisfied. Bask in your sense of fulfillment. Let yourself be overwhelmed with joy. You've found a kindred spirit and you've decided the two of you will become one.

Even the angels are giddy over it.

Did We Lose Our Girl?

What's it like to give your girl away to another man? Well, frankly, the whole concept seems a bit outdated. You weren't our girl to keep or give away in the first place. None of us own our children. We only rent them from God for twenty years or so and then we set them free. No one owns an adult.

There is a beautiful red cardinal in our backyard. Your mother feeds the feathered creature, but we have never thought of owning it. It flies into the yard; we enjoy it, and then it darts away again. Backyards don't have cages. Trees aren't covered with nets.

If I ever "lost" you, it was at your high school graduation. My eyes were damp and my throat was lumpy when they called your name. As the principal read aloud your honors and accomplishments and scholarships, I couldn't even see you through my misty eyes. I couldn't talk. (It's terribly awkward for a man to cry.)

It was the same feeling I had the night you performed in your last play. As you walked toward the floodlights and took your final bows I thought I would bawl like a baby.

In my heart that's when I said goodbye. I whispered farewell to my little girl.

From that day on you would become my friend. We would always look at each other as equals. Equals with a love so deep that nothing could ever wash it away.

Losing you to another man, that's small potatoes. No one is losing anything. You are stepping up to be united with a terrific person. The love of your life. That's nothing but happiness. What parent would want to pull you back and try to hold on to you? That would be like trying to put you back into Mrs. Darling's third grade class and your hair back in pigtails.

The best gifts God has for you are yet to come. You can begin to unwrap them today and tomorrow. And you can unwrap them with the man you adore.

What you and Phil share together as husband and wife is a relationship you and I could never have. And the relationship we enjoy as father and daughter is something you can't experience with Phil. Both of them are love, but they aren't the same. It's kind of like chocolate cake and ice cream. They aren't identical but both of them are terrific delights.

Move ahead. Time and nature and emotions and God's design all say the same thing. Move ahead into the fantastic life waiting for you. Nothing has been lost. Everything has been gained.

The Courage to Marry

*Y*ou'd never guess what I remember most about our wedding day. I was standing in the side room waiting for the ceremony to begin when I noticed an extra door. As the organ started playing I thought to myself, "I wonder if that door leads outside?"

Marriage is risky business. And it's a lot more risky today than it was back then. That's why I admire your courage to commit your whole life to someone even when marriages look shaky.

Refuse to marry? That would be like standing at the Grand Canyon and keeping

19

your eyes closed because you were afraid to look. Imagine a child who won't play in water because she might get wet. Marriage holds too much joy, too many hopes, too much happiness, too many laughs, too much life to shy away from it.

Marriage can have a dark side. There are too many broken hearts to pretend that marriage can't hurt. But those are just the stories that get our attention. We usually fail to notice the local newspaper announcements of fiftieth wedding anniversaries or the eighty-year-old neighbor who says she loves her husband more now than the day she married him.

The potential in marriage is enormous. It is like a treasure chest. Every year you open the lid more and more to discover rare jewels you wouldn't dare dream of. Pity the person who is afraid to even peek inside.

You aren't a stunt driver or an explorer. With your heart in one hand and your brain in the other, you're walking straight into a relationship close to the heart of God. You can enter it with your head held high, optimism beaming, and a smile big enough to make your cheeks hurt. Your tomorrows hold more promise than a sky painted with rainbows.

If you start to wonder what you're getting into, remember that happens to most of us. Anxiety comes with the wedding vows. That's all right.

But your love for this man will not be deterred by the marriage flutters. Every worthwhile endeavor has its bumpy roads.

Celebrate! You have made a fantastic decision. Take each day as it comes. Don't get bogged down in yesterday or try to leap ahead into tomorrow. This is the day that God has given for your life together to begin. Live it courageously.

Frogs and Princes

Try to imagine this: What if the man you marry never changes? Suppose he becomes frozen in time and always remains the same. Could you be as happy with him at age fifty-five as you are today?

Too many people get married believing that they can change their spouses. They believe in miracles, but unfortunately they think *they* are the miracle worker. It's nice to have that much faith in oneself, but they need a reality check.

Very seldom are any of us successful at changing someone else. Read that sentence again. The person you marry is basically the

22

❖

same one you will see across the breakfast table twenty or thirty years from now. Frogs don't turn into princes. Skunks stay skunks all of their lives. And, yes, angels tend to remain angels.

If anything, try to picture each of your partner's character traits increased by ten percent. People who are easily irritated while they are going together become more easily irritated after they get married. Bad tempers become fierce tempers within a year or two. Crude and rude have a way of degenerating into sloppy and obnoxious.

Only fairy princesses believe that they can take a self-centered guy, marry him, feed him, love him, give him lots of attention, and change him into a cool dude. But then fairy princesses still believe in spoofle dust, magic wands, and dancing elves.

Are there exceptions? Don't some wives change their husbands? Sure, but Halley's Comet comes around more often than that.

Love who you have. Work with him the way he is. Learn how to enhance his good qualities. Accept him lock, stock, and barrel and the two of you can become the great romance of the century.

Love his quirks. Don't struggle over the toothpaste tube. Get two tubes and squeeze your own however you like. If he spreads the Sunday newspaper all over the floor, be glad he's home to read it.

Never sweat the small stuff. And remember, most of our differences really are small stuff.

Make room for his foibles, habits, and peccadilloes. We all have them. You keep yours. Let him have his.

Dare to love him as he is. Love wears better when it is accepting, free of manipulation.

✻

A Question of Character

Of all the strengths you bring into a marriage, none is more valuable than your character. That may not sound as exotic as romance, wit, or charm, but character is the beam that holds the structure together. Without it marriage is little more than cotton candy or shifting winds.

Good character is never fickle. People who have it stand like rocks when the going gets tough. They aren't dependable one day and flaky tomorrow. They don't run like scared rabbits when the relationship starts to rattle. Character means we stay and

✧

stand even when we are down on each other.

Character takes its vows seriously. Very seriously. It still believes that a promise is a promise, a commitment a commitment, and that two people in love dedicate themselves to each other for life.

"In sickness and in health, for richer and for poorer" means what it suggests. Character doesn't believe marriage is a turnstile, a stop on the road, or a phase in life. Marriage isn't an experiment to dabble at to see if it works out.

Love isn't for irresponsible people. It isn't for the immature. Marriage wasn't created for those who can't tell time, keep appointments, call home, leave notes, or keep in touch. Love is too good to be wasted on independent souls. Only the truly interdependent know how to share meaningful affection. Only those who learn to blend reach true intimacy.

That's why we like your relationship with Phil. We think you realize what commitment is and you have the character needed to follow through. He seems like

❖

he's ready, too. People who don't want to "settle down" should never be talked into marrying. Settling down isn't for everyone. Marriage and independence are opposites. Compatibility comes only to those who want to "tie the knot" in the best sense of the term.

I can't say your mother and I never thought about leaving. She will have to speak for herself, but I've looked at my share of bus schedules and plane fares and have mulled over maps. Sometimes you wonder if it's worth hanging in there.

Why did we stay? Only God can answer that. But I'm glad we did. I'd like to think it's because most of the time we liked each other. We loved each other, too, but sometimes "like" is the determining factor. We enjoy each other's company.

On days we didn't appreciate each other God gave us the grace to reach back and pull up all the character we could muster. We determined to find a way to happiness again even if we had to break our necks.

Character means you made a deal. Character means you gave your word.

✧

Character means you give everything double effort when you need to. Character means if need be you will stand tall in the wind and the rain and the darkness, determined that you will see the light again.

※

Don't Forget Phil

*H*ow do brides manage to keep their cool at weddings? With photographs, flowers, and getting everyone into their tuxes and gowns, there's so much going on. But you didn't look tense.

Of course there was that little matter about Phil. Remember? Your husband? As the wedding hour came near, you got a phone call. It was Phil. In the hectic rush to look after all the details you forgot to stop by and pick up your groom!

It happens. You can't be expected to remember everything.

We have always admired your

independence. When you were growing up we spent most of our parental energies letting you go. You could handle most situations if everyone simply gave you free reign.

Now it's fun to watch you grow into *inter*dependence. Instead of merely creating your own head of steam and following it, you are meshing with the person you love. You aren't likely to lose your individuality. You've spent too many years cultivating your personality to simply let it all go now and cease to be June.

Your last name says a great deal: Coleman-Hull. A hyphenated name isn't for everyone, but it looks good on you. Gone are the days when a woman stopped existing because she married. Each of you is important, each of you is expressive, each of you is a dreamer, each of you is made in God's image.

Maybe it's like raisin bread. Without the raisins or without the bread, either way, you no longer have raisin bread. But the raisins will always be raisins and the bread will always be bread. Is the bread more important? Not if you want raisin bread.

❖

In marriage each person keeps his or her own identity. At the same time each is so intermingled with the other that they are one.

From now on, when I see your hyphenated name, I will think of raisin bread—separate ingredients blended together to form the desired whole.

The next time we get together we'd like to hear your thoughts on interdependence and individual identity. Come on over. And, by the way, don't forget to bring Phil.

Honeymoons and Shoofly Pie

$\mathscr{S}$ ome of the best marriages started off with rocky honeymoons. I've always wanted to get a group together and share "You won't believe what happened on our honeymoon" stories. So far I haven't found many others willing to bare their souls and swap accounts.

Our drive into marital bliss was beset by potholes. After the wedding, I changed clothes and threw our luggage into the car trunk. As I walked to the driver's side, I tore my trousers on the edge of the rear bumper.

❖

I entered the motel lobby in Rockville, Maryland, half crouched over, holding the front of my trousers.

I had told myself a hundred times to sign the register "Mr. and Mrs." You guessed it. I signed my own name.

Excited and nervous, we went to our room and began to change clothes and take turns in the bathroom. I came out to discover my exhausted bride sound asleep. I settled into a chair, turned on the TV and pouted while I watched the late movie. (This is the first time I've admitted to this small glitch in our trip to matrimonial bliss.)

The next day we drove to the Pocono Mountains. We stayed at a beautiful resort with a huge fireplace and a large four-poster bed. Whatever energy we may have lacked the previous night we more than compensated for that evening.

When the sun arose, we didn't. Around midmorning Pat grew faint and we realized we had forgotten to eat. Begrudgingly, we pulled ourselves together and went for breakfast. Then we purchased a large shoofly pie. We took it back to our room hoping we wouldn't have to leave again for a day or two.

A couple of days later, Pat and I discovered the delightful town of Scranton and a local theater showing *Music Man*.

Don't be surprised or distracted by whatever happens on your honeymoon. Most honeymoons work out very well. Very well indeed.

I'll Talk to the Lord

Frequently we have opportunity to tell our friends how you are getting along. They remember you well and wonder what you're up to. Often they stop me in the store, at church, or on the street and ask about you. Just the other day, Marge asked me to say hello but I forgot to do that.

I don't tell them everything because they aren't asking for a biography. Proudly, though, I do tell them a couple of the things going on in your life. They always seem so happy for you.

The number one friend I talk to about you and your new husband, of course, is the

Lord. Naturally, He knows all the facts. He already knew about the month when you guys were broke. Even the argument you had wasn't news to Him.

I don't talk to the Lord to fill Him in on all the events. Instead I give Him my wish list. I tell Him what good experiences I would like to see in your life. Seldom does the list consist of objects, though it could. Mostly I ask God about more important needs. I find myself asking the Lord to give you things like:

a sense of peace

physical protection

the freedom to forgive

a growing concept of love

patience with yourself and others

the wisdom to do, without overdoing

a close walk with Christ

tears of happiness

one day at a time

the ability to become one with Phil as he becomes one with you.

Not only do I ask, but I also find myself committing. Your safety, your marriage, your jobs, your health, and your future are more than I can handle. So I won't try. I'll ask the Lord to be in charge while I sleep the whole night through.

I promise not to pray for you out of habit. Neither will I pray because of guilt. I pray for a better reason than fear. I talk to the Lord about you because of love. Convinced that prayer makes a big difference, I want to talk to my Friend about you and your marriage.

Ten Percent Change

*D*on't get your hopes up that you can change someone else. Trying to change ourselves takes a Herculean effort. Attempting to change others is flirting with insanity.

The big thing I would have changed about your mother is obvious to everyone who knows us. I wanted her to stay up late at night and share my appreciation for life after ten o'clock. That was my dream for the first decade and a half of our marriage.

I pictured Pat and I playing games, reading, and watching the late movie until the stroke of midnight. Then we would bound off to bed like love doves during mating season. Somewhere along the way the dream went south, leaving a sleepy bird and a frustrated bird behind.

Not that she didn't try. She was a real trooper. She took naps, downed caffeinated coffee, and propped herself up in a hardback chair. But no matter how hard she tried, around ten o'clock her head nodded, her eyelids slid downward, and her lower jaw dropped like a bridge.

She was gone.

And there I was. Left to lament a lonely evening parked next to my slumbering wife. Silently, I grumbled to myself while she traveled through dreamland.

One day, by the grace of God, it occurred to me that it must be terribly difficult for Pat to try and stay up late. If I had to go to bed early every night, I would be owly and disjointed and unpleasant. It would be fighting nature. It would be like teaching a seal how not to swim.

That's when I quit. Pat has every right to be Pat. Just as I have every right to be Bill.

✧

We may change our partners by five to ten percent. They should be discouraged from slurping soup and eating frosting off the cake. In the first couple of weeks of marriage, every spouse should be trained to pick up his own socks and skivvies. If one partner isn't used to calling home when he or she is going to be late, a training session is in order.

Thoughtfulness and courtesy are traits well worth pursuing. Beyond that don't expect too many meaningful changes. Living room lizards can learn to fly but only if they want to. Negative thinkers become positive thinkers only at their own pace.

When change comes a person likes to think it was his own idea. Those changes are most likely to last.

I could go on and on about this, but I need to turn out the light—my love dove's asleep.

Don't s About Sex

*O*ne of the first things you will notice about marriage is that sex plays a significant role. For a while it plays the leading role.

Though we don't claim to be experts on the subject, we have found some advice worthy of following. Please pardon our boldness as we pass along some important information on this vital aspect of your marriage.

THE THREE "DON'TS" ABOUT SEX

Don't answer the phone or doorbell.
It's amazing how many couples stop

41

what they are doing because of a buzzer, clanker, or bell. Now a smoke alarm I might understand, but a telephone? Can sex be so boring that you would interrupt it to chat on the phone? Would you really rather talk to the magazine salesperson at the door?

Don't worry about syncopation.

Too many couples think they have to orgasm together or the sex isn't worth anything. Where do these stories start? It's great to orgasm together. It's also great to orgasm at different times. It's even okay if only one partner reaches a climax.

The important thing is that both of you end up satisfied. If this wasn't a good time for you to climax, so be it. Hit it on the next go-round.

Our number one goal is to make the earth move for the other person. If we do that, we will probably cash in, too. Make sure each of you hits the jackpot every time you want to hit it.

Don't be trendy.

Like most behavior, sex can become faddish. We read about how many times the average couple does it and we think we

❖

need to match that number. We wonder if what we do measures up to the sexual practices of the general population.

Ignore all of that and go for sex on your own terms. If you make each other happy, you don't have to answer to anyone else.

Sex is good. Sex is great. It may be one of the Lord's better inventions. Never let it suffer from neglect.

Learn to Love the Giants

*I*f you haven't done this yet, do it today. Turn to the sports page and go
find your husband. Ask Phil to explain the
baseball box scores. Boys grow up reading
them and men continue the tradition most
of their lives.

Men never feel more manly than when
they are explaining the intricacies of sports
to their ladies. Let him tell you what ERA
really means. It's not the Equal Rights
Amendment. Then go down the column to
see who has the most RBI's. Some of us real
men call them Ribees. You will also need to
know how to calculate a baseball player's

batting average and what it means. If he's batting .210, that means he's going back to Toledo. If he's batting .326 he's probably going to Cooperstown. Toledo and Cooperstown are a million miles apart. Phil can explain that, too.

Don't ask him what the infield fly rule is, however. Even we he-men have to look that one up.

Buy him a set of baseball cards. Not just any cards. He's a San Francisco Giants fan. And don't give him the cards unless you have plenty of time, because he's going to read them to you. Every statistic on every card of every player. How many at-bats, how many games, how many walks, how many strikeouts as well as how many hot dogs each player ate.

Men don't want you to know as much about sports as they do. They might feel threatened by that. They merely want you to share a little interest.

Once a year go to a ball game with your husband. Eat a hot dog and don't complain about the fat content. Eat some nachos and don't mention the cholesterol. Drink a cold

✧

cola and tell him it's yummy delicious.

While you are sitting in the ball park listening to the crack of the bat, watching the scoreboard light up, or standing during the seventh-inning stretch, just once yell, "Throw the bum out!" Do all of this and your husband will know you love him.

❖

Power Struggles

f I talk to a person or a group about marriage battles, the responses are almost always the same: The three things most couples fight over are money, children, and sex. Our feelings run strong on those personal, intimate subjects. So we have trouble compromising to reach solutions to our disagreements.

During the past couple of years husbands and wives have found a fourth reason to climb into the marital boxing arena. Couples now also fight over power: Who is in charge around here? Who gets their way most of the time? Who gets the final vote?

47

Power struggles undoubtedly are a leading cause of divorce. Each spouse takes his corner of the ring and leers across at the other. Occasionally they meet in the center of the ring to exchange blows then quickly return to the safety of their corners.

Some marriages survive this kind of sparring. Unfortunately, after each round the partners come away with psychological and spiritual bruises.

We jokingly call marriage "a license to fight." Often we do need to argue, debate, air our opinions. But when the discussion is over, we have to sign a treaty and keep it.

Most couples don't need to fight as much as they need to clinch.

Give up the power struggle early. It's actually a sign of fragile egos trying to prove their worth. Imagine an immature adult attempting to find self-esteem by winning. Our self-worth is never established by victories over others.

Struggles are real. Every couple has them. If there are no struggles, is it because they are identical personalities or because one person totally dominates the other?

Neither situation sounds healthy.

The goal of a good marriage struggle is to reach satisfying compromises. He wants to vacation at a biker's convention and she has a beach in mind. How do they find a solution where each person wins? Can they find a biker's convention at Myrtle Beach? How about a biker's convention this year, and surf and sand the next?

A need to beat our partner places everyone in a win/lose situation. That's a bad place to be. Aim instead for as many win/win situations as possible.

When one partner says, "I want to do it because you want to do it," that's a win/win deal!

I went with Pat to a Garrison Keillor concert because she thinks he's clever and funny. She went with me to hear Willie Nelson. What a marriage! Neither of us struggled over it. We just clinched a lot.

❖

Faithfulness and Integrity

*H*ow much the world has changed. People committed adultery in previous generations. Adultery isn't an invention ushered in by the computer age or home videos. When I was a child I couldn't help but notice the young lady across the street. When her husband was away serving in the Navy, a number of men came to her door. But who am I to say they weren't salesmen replenishing her Fuller brush supply?

The number of people involved in adultery might actually be no greater today. But there is a difference. Today people discuss whether adultery is wrong. Yesterday, when people did it, they knew it was wrong.

Not long ago, a prominent American declared the Ten Commandments outdated. And what is outdated about them? Is it the prohibition against stealing? The restriction on murder? Should we covet our neighbor's house and wife? Is adultery okay?

It's confusing to think that many people indulge in it. Some presidents do it. People in congress do it. Entertainers do it. The butcher, the baker, and ministers do it. Some writers defend them and say it's all right to have another's spouse.

None of us know what we might do in times of temptation. All of us are fragile. All of us sin. All of us have moments when we don't want to hold the moral line.

But given our weaknesses, let us get one thing straight: Adultery is wrong. Faithfulness and fidelity are right. Unfaithfulness is a violation of our sacred trust in each other. It is never right to have sex outside of that marriage trust—with another person's marriage partner, or with someone not yet married.

I feel foolish even discussing it. I am surprised that not everyone knows adultery is wrong. I'm sad that some feel this is up for debate.

This isn't your problem. And yet it is. It is easy to be swayed by the claims of popular morality. But remember: Some truths are eternal, and marriage fidelity is meant to last forever.

Of those who commit adultery, most never do it again. Adultery is one of those acts that should haunt and unsettle us. By the grace of God, the action is even forgivable. But adultery is definitely wrong.

And why is it wrong? Is it God's attempt to keep us from a good time? Quite the contrary. It is His loving way of protecting our relationships for the truly great times.

The Oil of Joy

*I*f the hinges on your front door start to squeak, get a can of oil and apply a few drops. The door will soon swing with quiet ease.

When the car door becomes hard to open, get out the oil can again and aim it at strategic locations. Watch out afterward. The door will become so loose that it might swing back and hit you as you get out of the car.

A dab of oil at the right time and in the right place takes the creaks, squeaks, croaks, rasps, and grating out of all manner of hinges. Never be without an oil can somewhere around the house.

The Bible tells about another kind of oil that takes the squeaks out of relationships. It's called the oil of joy. This is one of my favorite passages. It says God has blessed you "by anointing you with the oil of joy" (Psalm 45:7).

Picture a clay jar from Bible times. In your mind pick up the jar by the handles and tilt it forward. Try to imagine joy pouring out the spout.

Joy is a gift from God. He furnishes us with plenty of reasons to enjoy life. He gives us satisfaction beyond measure. All you have to do is tilt the jar and pour joy over each area of your marriage.

Too many couples pour moodiness, gloom, and competitiveness over their relationship. Instead of taking out the squeaks, they merely add to the difficulties. They get sand in the gears, which raises a terrible raucous and brings the marriage machine to a near halt.

Joy keeps the cogs rolling smoothly. Joy speeds up the mechanism and keeps the engine humming.

BEFORE I GIVE YOU AWAY

❖

I don't always have a choice, but when I do, I can choose to apply joy to my relationship. Too much routine and tension interfere with a smooth marriage.

Since God has been generous enough to supply joy, we should be sensible enough to use it. Before this day is out, see how many places you can squirt a little joy around the house.

Spiritual Growth

The two of you are such active Christians that I know spiritual reality and connections are very important to you. Plenty of people want to tell you how to have spiritual unity, victory, and success in your marriage. Everyone seems to have six steps, four keys, or ten points. There's enough advice out there, so I won't add any magic formulas of my own.

However, if I had one bit of encouragement to offer, it would be to carve out your own spiritual growth. The Father, the Son, and the Holy Spirit, each and all, want to interact with you and will always welcome you into free and glad communication.

When your mother and I come to visit, we hope you will do as you please about praying before we eat. Don't try to accommodate us or change your habits for fear of what we expect. When you come to our house, we decide when to pray and when not to. We read or don't read according to our comfort zone. We hope you will live within your spiritual zone, too.

If you don't care to pray before you eat, I'll still eat just as much. On the other hand, if you want to pray or chant, ring bells or sing, I'm happy to eat that way also. I want to be in your home, in your atmosphere, and fit in with your values. I'd hate to think you changed them to appease your fragile father.

When it comes to personal prayer and Scripture reading, have the courage to walk your own path. Your mother and I have seldom read the Bible or prayed together in the thirty years we've been married. We're different people. Different speeds. Different temperaments. (You've probably noticed.) We find it easier to drink from the spiritual well each at our own pace.

Some books, speakers, and seminar leaders tell you that couples should pray together. Maybe. But "should" is too strong for me. I've always been suspicious of others who tell me what my spiritual life should look like. Instead, listen to teachers who explain what spiritual life *could* be.

Together. Apart. A little bit of each. Whatever mix helps you walk closer to Christ.

Take a pledge that you won't let your relationship with God turn into guilt. Guilt is a real bummer. Spirituality is a blessing. Those who grow in it find warm communication with the Lord. Anyone who doesn't is missing a vital link. Guilt isn't the issue. Inner peace and strength and intimacy through the Spirit are the real benefits.

Bless His Parents

Someone has said we expect too much of marriage. We want it to erase all of our past shortcomings and to fulfill all of our dreams for tomorrow. Unfortunately, marriage wasn't designed to accomplish either of those goals. Partners have to be real and recognize the severe limitations present in any relationship.

It helps if we enter marriage with as little baggage as possible. Though we all bring some quirks, hang-ups, and psychological twitches into the relationship, the fewer the better.

It's not impossible for people from con-

❖

torted backgrounds to make excellent spouses. It may take more time and work, but they often turn out to be outstanding partners. However, those with loving parents and a godly example seem to have an easier time all around.

That's one more reason why you will want to bless the name of Phil's parents. They have put a great deal of energy and dedication into caring for their son. He might have acquired his good character on his own, but knowing his parents, it's easy to recognize the godly influence they have been in his life.

In the frenzy of our own lives, too many of us forget our partner's family. Phil's parents prayed, hoped, invested, persevered, trained, and remained faithful to a son they so obviously love. They shared the Christ they worship, follow, and serve. Their faith is the cornerstone of their existence.

Now that you have the prize, remember where it originated. Salute those who crafted, polished, and guarded it. Phil is his own person, a product of his own choices, a development of his own gifts and talents.

And yet his parents have left their indelible mark on him.

Honor his mother and father. Continue to show them great respect. Try not to take them for granted. Your allegiance is to each other now, but never forget the fortified nest from which he came.

Keep in touch with them. Think of ways to show them how much you appreciate them. And, sometimes, in the midst of leading your own lives, tell them what a fantastic job they have done.

Bless Phil's parents all of their lives. . . because they have given of themselves to bless the two of you.

Changing Together

*H*usbands and wives change continually throughout their years together. Originally we had a traditional idea of marriage, career, and home. Pat was going to stay home and care for the children, while I took a steady job and paid the bills.

Times change, sometimes rapidly. Most couples no longer wash diapers, eat 95% of their meals at home, have one car, or live on acreages. Smart people know when to change with the times and when not to.

You and your husband will change. That's the good news and the sometimes scary news. Change is dynamic. The trick is

✧

trying to keep up with your spouse and change together rather than change apart. Dolphins can either swim together or drift off alone. People can do the same.

As both of your interests become more varied, will you be able to establish enough similar interests? Keep an eye on your time together. If you notice it is dwindling, take a reality check. Sit down together and express your concerns. Talk about making adjustments. Discover new things the two of you could enjoy together.

Long ago and far away, we used to think that adapting was a wife's job. If she felt her husband was finding new interests, she would scurry after him and blend into his world. Today we know better. Each partner has an obligation to fit into the other's world.

But it isn't necessary for it to become a gender issue. Don't pout over who should make the first move. That's territorial. Nations and animals can afford to fight over turf, but couples can't.

Speak up early if you feel like you are changing apart too much:

"We're starting to drift."

"Let's head for the harbor."

"Let's not let the fog set in."

Change is not the problem. Change is good. Thirty years from now you won't be the same person you are today nor should you be. And yet some things never change.

The problem comes when you fail to grow and change together. It isn't easy. If you have children in the future, they could become your world, while Phil's world keeps expanding beyond the home. Husbands need to put their energy back into the home while wives need opportunities to grow beyond those walls.

It's an exciting time to be married. The two of you have the opportunity to carve out your own tomorrow—together.

✳

Married and Lonely

 ou did it. You found someone you wanted to become one with and have by your side for the rest of your life. None of your past friends could fill your world as completely or as satisfactorily as Phil. He is a presence, a nearness, an all-engulfing love. Like the songwriter says, he "fills up your senses."

Despite all of the closeness you two will experience, it is still possible to feel lonely. Be careful if you feel yourself falling backward into mental isolation. Too often a married person doesn't sense that he is a part of his partner. That feeling might have

65

nothing to do with the facts.

Surely you have had that feeling in a crowd or at a party—people surround you, talking, laughing, even asking you questions, but you picture yourself outside of the group. Twenty people crowding in on you, and yet you feel lonely.

If that happens in marriage, and it happens to most of us some time or other, don't blame the relationship. Your marriage could be flourishing but still do nothing to ease your lonely feelings.

Loneliness is a personal problem. It has little to do with how many people are around us or who they are. Loneliness is created by our lack of satisfaction with ourselves. Some things marriage cannot cure, no matter how loving one's partner may be.

Often lonely people are at war inside themselves with:

their spouse

others

God

themselves.

The cure for loneliness is found inside

your heart. If you want to live above it, you can begin by:

1. Accepting your spouse as he is.
2. Helping others so you aren't so self-centered.
3. Moving closer to God's Holy Spirit.
4. Liking yourself for who you are.

These four steps are moves we can make to overcome the battles.

My guess is you don't struggle a lot with loneliness. And I think the reason is that you have found some measure of peace in all four of these realms. But no one stays on top all the time.

When feelings of loneliness come around and make you feel sorry for yourself, don't be too quick to blame your marriage. Usually marriage is not the culprit. Instead, look inside your heart and ask yourself how things are going in these four potential battlefields.

Reaching Intimacy

*I*ntimacy has become a euphemism for sex. Someone may wonder if two people have been "intimate." That's a euphemism for "slept together," which is yet another euphemism.

Because we avoid straight talk, the word "intimate" becomes meaningless. The fact is that a couple can have sex for years and never reach intimacy. They may participate in a wonderful physical act; they may have received a great deal of pleasure, and still they could remain all but strangers.

Intimacy is the ability to disclose who we are to someone else. We become intimate as we learn to read another's mind, heart, and soul and let him read ours. Intimacy is transparency. We need to be able to see through each other.

That's one of the most frightening parts of marriage. Sometimes we are afraid to share everything because our partner will be able to see through us. The couple who opens up and allows each spouse to see and be seen has a chance of reaching true intimacy.

Intimacy is risky.

Intimacy is painful.

Intimacy is satisfying.

Intimacy takes time.

Not many of us walk up to someone and expose our psyche. All of us hold back, protect, and distort ourselves. The more we are able to stop hiding from our spouse, the more open and fulfilling marriage can be.

It takes time. People who are divorced within their first year of marriage never really knew each other.

People are like whiskey barrels. If you let an empty whiskey barrel sit for a long time, the whiskey that has absorbed into the wood will slowly give itself up. As much as a gallon could be retrieved from one seemingly empty barrel.

There is a great deal about us that lies dormant within the walls of our lives. It takes time for the full person to "drain out" so our partner can collect it.

Some couples who have been married twenty-five years still have trouble knowing each other. For some reason they don't want to reveal their true identities.

The Bible says that in marriage the two of you become one. A large part of how one you become is determined by the level of intimacy you reach.

Make these goals yours in marriage: transparency, disclosure, and intimacy. In your own way, at your own speed, give yourselves to each other and become the ultimate in oneness.

❖

Who Makes You Happy?

*H*ere is some instant wisdom, which takes the average person a decade or longer to learn through experience. While a person is learning this, she is likely to make many mistakes and suffer an endless array of heartaches.

I wish someone had told me: *I am responsible for my own happiness.*

The big delusion of marriage is that my spouse takes on the job of making me happy. Too many of us think marriage is an ocean cruise. Once we get on deck we expect our partners to entertain us, feed us, say clever things, and generally keep us amused.

That approach to marriage is heading for shipwreck. My spouse cannot be held accountable for my level of satisfaction.

Children tell their mothers, "There's nothing to do." They expect their parents to do magic tricks and make happiness appear. Smart moms refuse to play recreation director. They let children devise their own forms of activity.

When we get married, we should be old enough to realize that life isn't this way. My spouse won't become my mother. I can't expect my partner to break out the blocks or drag out the toy box simply because I am bored.

If I am depressed, disgusted, discouraged, and my imagination is as dull as unbuttered toast, my spouse is not obligated to rescue me from a listless evening. I am responsible for my feelings. I am responsible for my behavior. I am responsible for my attitudes.

Hopefully my spouse will be able to

jump in and play in my sandbox. But she can't always. She won't always. Adults shouldn't start pouting because their partner doesn't drop everything to build sand castles.

My spouse will make me happy. That's the good news. But it's not her main job. Personal satisfaction is my own responsibility.

When my spouse is busy, cranky, tired, self-centered, or involved in chess tournaments, my personal satisfaction is first, last, and always my own business. If that's not the case, I become a little child again, pouting because someone else doesn't produce.

That is misplaced pressure. Grab your own brass ring. Make your own day count. If the two of you can make the day work together, all the better. But never feel like "a day without my spouse is a day at the dump." Most days are as good as you are willing to make them.

❖

Thirteen Guidelines for Squeezing

  Recently some of my friends have come to refer to their partners as their "squeeze." One of the vital elements in any good marriage is the fine art of squeezing, yet little has been written about the subject. The word squeeze means "to handclasp" or "to embrace." After years of research in our own relationship, I have been able to refine squeezing to a few dependable guidelines.

  These guidelines are addressed to men, but women can learn from them as well.

Feel free to add to the list as you learn new squeezing techniques in your marriage.

13 Guidelines for
Successful Squeezing

1. Buy two tubes of toothpaste and squeeze yours any way you choose.
2. Never squeeze her when she is carrying something hot.
3. Never squeeze too hard.
4. If she says don't squeeze—don't.
5. If she squeezes back, keep squeezing.
6. If she says squeeze here, squeeze her there.
7. If you squeeze in public, be polite.
8. If you squeeze in private, be personal.
9. If you squeeze in bed, be prepared.
10. Never squeeze half a grapefruit.
11. Never squeeze while she's angry.
12. Never squeeze when she first comes home (probably heading for the facility).
13. Never squeeze when she's late for something.

❖

I had a good friend who was an outstanding accordion player. He once told me that in twenty years of squeezing the accordion, not once did it squeeze back. Squeezing back is very important.

❧

An Elephant in the Pantry

very time you walk by, you can hear it. Sometimes it's shuffling its feet or pushing against the door. Once in a while you hear the beast raise its head and give a frightening roar.

Despite the noises and the obvious menace, each of you walks by without doing anything. Often you even go out of your way to avoid it.

Each of you is perfectly aware of the elephant in the pantry, but you pretend it isn't there. The facts are hard to ignore, but you

✧

manage to succeed. If people visit, they are suspicious. They can hear the rattling around and are certain something is wrong.

Often a couple has an elephant in the pantry, but they refuse to deal with the facts. They have something they need to face. Something they need to discuss. The pantry door has to be opened, the monster must be set free and the space has to be aired out.

Most marriages have them—an area or two or ten that need to be talked over. Instead of confronting reality, couples leave the door shut and act like the problem doesn't exist.

Believe it or not, some things don't need to be discussed. Not every small issue has to be dragged out, examined, hashed, rehashed, and resolved. Some things have to be let go. I feel sorry for couples who turn every slight into a Harvard debate. They rant and rave over the toothpaste tube, the toilet seat, the cereal box, the newspaper on the chair, and whether he eats the ice cream before he eats the pie.

What's the harm? If he changes the

channel on the TV every 30 seconds or if she uses half a bottle of ketchup at every meal, big deal. Give it a rest. Too many young couples looking for perfect communication nitpick until it's painful for them to spend an evening together.

Forgive each other and adjust as much as possible. Marriage is a love feast, not a ten-round welterweight boxing match.

But once in a while a difference between you becomes too much. The problem festers and grows and sprouts entirely out of proportion to its real significance. Then it becomes the baby elephant in the pantry. Left alone the elephant will feed, gain weight, and become mammoth.

Don't let that happen. Once you feel a little problem starting to grow tusks, go for it right away. Open the door and expose the old pachyderm for what it is becoming.

Talk about it before the leathery skinned behemoth tears the house down.

The Healing Power in Marriage

*A*ll of us are wounded. Wounds are part of the human condition. We wish we didn't have them. We think it's unfair that we are injured. Sometimes we are angry at God because He didn't protect us from harm. A lot goes on in our minds and hearts when we are hurting.

Some wounds are a surface variety. Others are deeply internal. These can't be seen by others, but they are terribly painful.

When we get married, we hope that married life can heal us. It certainly has medicinal properties. Cheerfulness, pleasure, hope, newness, faith, challenge, purpose, love, tenderness, humor, and companionship are balms and salves, especially for the soul.

Marriage is an infirmary. We reach out and touch each other in a way that brings health. Many hurts are best cured by someone holding us in their arms.

Marriage cures surface wounds. Real and painful, but surface nevertheless. Deep wounds are occasionally healed, but when they are, it is after a decade or two or three of marriage.

Deep wounds often need the help of a specialist. They are frequently entangled, complex, and destructive. Many marriages don't last long enough to help. Others drag on without ever seeing the wounded one reach genuine wholeness.

If you have deep wounds, get help and get it soon. Don't let it sap the health from your relationship.

When it comes to the normal cuts and bruises of the soul, this is a chance to play doctor. Playing doctor in marriage can be great fun.

Hold him. Slowly, patiently, lovingly stroke him. Act as if you have all the time in the world. Block out everything else. There is no obligation as important as healing your spouse.

Listen to him. What is he saying and what does he mean? What are his fears and what makes him angry? What ingredients are boiling and bubbling inside?

Reassure him. Doctors of the soul are also good encouragers. Remind him how much confidence you have in him. Tell him he is God's wonderful gift to you. Let him know how much he is wanted and needed.

When I married, I didn't understand love. I didn't trust love. I rejected it. I was bogged down in confusion. Patiently, your mother healed me by showing me what love could do. God gave us spouses as doctors of our souls.

An Unusual
Mating Call

Surely you have heard of this bird, with its most unusual mating call. Normally one expects a bird to whistle or chirp or hoot or screech. But this bird has a peculiar sound. Found all over the world, this famous fowl is known as the Yellow Bellied Whiner. On a quiet evening you can hear this call echoing through the trees:

"If he really loved me he would . . ."

The call tapers off at the end and even the best-trained ornithologist is unable to make out the last few words. A much touted

theory among birders is that the Yellow Bellied Whiner does not want its mate to hear
the end of the sentence. It believes the
mate should be able to guess what it has in
mind.

An identical problem exists among married birds of a feather. I want something
from my mate but I don't want to tell her
what it is. I think that if she really loved me
she would know what I want. It's as if I expect my partner to be a psychic or a palm
reader.

Yellow Bellied Whiners never say what
they want to watch on television. They seldom say where they want to eat. Sometimes
the little feathered creatures are so deceit-
ful that they say they want nothing for Valentine's Day when they don't actually mean
it. They expect their mates to understand
that "No" means "Yes."

They hide in the hedges to make themselves hard to see, and then they get angry
if their mates don't see them.

Don't be a member of this coy flock. Let
Phil know what rows your boat. And be specific. If your idea of a good time is kite fly-

ing in the park, please let him know. If you want to join the local couples tug-o-war team, speak up. As Hank Williams sang a long time ago, "Tell me what in the world you want me to do."

Many wives are too timid to say what they need. They believe in humility, in giving to their husbands, in not complaining, in not demanding. Unfortunately, they turn into passive partners who often pout because their husbands don't guess what they want.

Tonight, when Phil gets home, say to him, "I want to go out to eat at the Belching Bovine and I want to do it now." Surely he'll thank you for revealing your true passion.

If he wants to know where you got this idea, let him guess.

The Best Gift

*J*ewelry boxes are nice. Pat still has the one I gave her while we were dating. Rings are good. Pat still has those, too. But as valuable and meaningful as these gifts are, they don't come close to the most important present I can give my spouse.

The best gift I can give to my marriage partner is a good healthy sense of myself. A right sense of self-worth and self-acceptance will be the grand prize of any relationship.

People with a low opinion of themselves busily put themselves down and act like they are mud. They have little hope of ever being equal with the person they love. Mud cannot contribute meaningfully to a marriage.

Others act like Greek heroes. They think they are too good for the average bloke. Even inside their hearts they strut around as if they are superior. A satisfying relationship is impossible when partners think they are better than their spouses.

Mud-people cannot open up and show intimacy. They are too frightened. Greek hero types can't open up because they are afraid to show their vulnerable side. But people in the middle, those with a good healthy sense of self, are prepared to open up and become intimate with someone else.

The best gift you and your husband will ever give to each other is a sense of reasonable confidence. A resolve that whatever kick in the head the two of you might take, you can bounce back and deal with it by the grace of God. That confidence finds its anchor in the love of Jesus Christ, but it is confidence nevertheless.

Do what it takes to build your mind,

✧

your courage, and your spirit. Exercise, take classes, pray, get counseling, read books, learn a new language. Branch out, get experience, find friends who will give you positive feedback. Life is filled with struggles, and you need to be in good shape for whatever comes your way.

No one wants a partner who is a wimp. Stay in training. Relationships become lop-sided and deficient if one person mentally drops out.

A spouse receives confidence from her partner as she feeds confidence to him. You will always be glad that you contributed to your relationship as an equal.

❖
The School of Marriage

When I ask newlyweds to tell me the one thing they would like to get out of marriage, they act as though they are frightened to death. They don't want to say what it is. Are they afraid they will sound selfish, demanding, complaining? Is it too risky to speak up and say what you want or need?

Marriage has to mature to the place where each person can let his needs be known. Partners in the habit of suppressing their desires travel rocky roads and often end up in the ditch.

Look at marriage like a classroom. Even

a laboratory. Each of you is a professor. Your job is to teach your husband how to make this partnership satisfying for you. His task is to teach you what makes marriage click for him. You are the best authorities on what love means to you.

If you don't speak up, your partner has to guess what you need. That's cruel. Terrible tension builds when spouses try to guess what the other needs. Will this make her happy? Is he going to hate that? Will this send her into a tizzy?

Pat and I had just visited a large restored home in Kansas. We had listened to a long spiel about the gas lighting system, the rugs from France, and the fascinating dumbwaiter. While the guide painstakingly described the upstairs windows, I distinctly remember thinking that I should pray for a seizure.

On the way out of the building, I turned and asked Pat to help me.

"On a scale of one to ten, how much did you enjoy this tour?"

"About a two," she replied.

"Well, I'd give it a one on a good day," I added.

All the time I thought Pat loved overstuffed mansions. Now I find out she thought it was an obsession of mine! I couldn't believe we had rumbled around scores of old structures each thinking we were sacrificing so the other could get their kicks.

We haven't toured a home since.

School was in session on the steps of that old mansion. Pat taught me. I taught Pat. We each got an education.

None of us needs to be rude or dictatorial, but we do need to educate. Tell him what greases your wheels and what gums up your axles. Ask him what churns his butter and what clogs up his drain.

Make marriage a practical classroom.

❖

What Is Money?

*I*t is very rare that you find two people who totally agree on money. The subject is a sore spot for most couples, and seldom do they handle it well. There are three reasons why cash, credit, debt, and saving are so painful for marriages.

    1. We don't talk about money.
    2. We don't agree on its purpose.
    3. We spend at different rates.

Take a close look at each of these.

One, we don't talk about money.

Many couples say money is all they do talk about. More precisely, finances are what they argue over, not what they talk about.

If you aren't careful, your once romantic, exciting future will degenerate into one continuous battle over utility bills, taxes, and installment loans. Talk, plan, budget, and keep on talking, planning, and budgeting. It takes work to gain control of our finances, but the effort is worth it.

Two, we don't agree on the purpose.

That's all right. We don't have to agree. But we do have to understand how the other feels. Is money evil? Is it good? Is it security? Is it power? Is it freedom? Is it opportunity? Is it service to others? Is it yours? Is it an offering to God?

The answer isn't as simple as it might appear. There are no right or wrong answers. There is some truth to be seen in each of these descriptions of money. People from different backgrounds and different experiences see the purpose of money from different angles.

Money is a force. It is not dormant. Money is like having a pet snake. It might be okay to have around, but everyone needs to know where it is.

Three, we spend at different rates.

You've probably noticed that already. My guess is you two have been used to shopping at different types of stores. You probably won't agree on the types of restaurants, clothes, or furnishings you prefer at first either. Maybe you never will agree completely. That's all right. You can each adjust.

As time passes, you may discover that your spouse saves or spends in his own way. So do you. That's where talking and compromise are important. Aim for the middle road. Save for tomorrow and enjoy today. Too much of either will leave something or someone hurting.

Be your own couple. Make money a friend instead of an enemy.

Low Love Days

*I*t happens to everyone. Some days you won't feel like you're in love. All of us have blue Mondays sometimes, and we can have them any day of the week. The sky is overcast, our brain is thick as syrup, and our body is sluggish. Then to top it off our spouse says something dumb like, "What happened to your hair?" or "I thought you finished that last week."

Sometimes even the kindest of us forget to think. We say the wrong things at the worst times and hurt our partner's feelings. It's not that we're mean people, it's just hard to be thoughtful all the time.

On the days when the love temperature dips particularly low, when the mercury sits on the bottom like a stone in the lake, remind yourself of this: love knows how to rebound. One day of love on the limp doesn't mean it's over. Limping love learns how to walk again, to run, to leap, and even to do cartwheels.

Love seldom travels a level highway. It battles steep climbs and then races downhill for a while. Love turns to the left and then swings back at the next curve. For days, maybe weeks, love runs at top speed. Then it meets a couple of detours, a few miles of rocky road, a stretch of minimum maintenance, and it could possibly park for a day or two.

But on the day when you wonder where love has gone, try to remember this is normal. A day or two, a week or two of dullness doesn't mean it's time to call the mortician. You may spend months or more wondering how much electricity is in this love machine. Fortunately, it will flow again and the sparks will start to fly.

My Lord is the Lord of hope. He is

faithful through times of despair, but His eye is always on encouragement. Sometimes when love seems to have died and we don't see any way to slap it back into reality, the best thing, the only thing, is to commit it to the Lord.

The prayer during these dry spells goes something like this:

"Lord, I don't have the energy it takes to work on this. The light at the end of the tunnel is seriously fogged over. Please keep me close to you. Keep me in your arms until I am back in his arms again. Soon. Amen."

It really works.

How to Get Your
Husband's Ear

*I*t often takes years to figure out how
to communicate effectively with a
husband. Most of this process is accom-
plished through trial and error, hit and
miss, success and failure. You will probably
follow that same pattern as you learn how
to communicate with Phil.

Usually couples start off talking a great
deal. Then after a few months reality sets
in, and you both fall into a normal routine.
Too often "normal routine" means you talk
less and less.

❖

Every husband is different and yet they tend to be the same. There are a few tried and proven guidelines that could speed up the communication process. Give these a try. If they work, your marriage is way ahead. If they don't work, you don't have to say who gave them to you.

1. Give him choices.

Men hate to feel like they aren't allowed to make decisions. Suggest that you would like to go out Thursday or Friday. (Sometimes you can't because the symphony is only performing on Thursday, but give him an option whenever possible.)

2. Ask specific questions.

Don't—don't—don't ask "How did work go today?" Nothing is more likely to get a one word answer ("fine"). Narrow it down to, "Did you have fun with the new computer?" or "How is that project coming along?"

3. Try upbeat starters.

Don't begin a conversation with a depressing subject. Instead, something like "How do you think the football team will do Saturday?" will be a golden intro for many

❖

men. "I see Carlton got voted into the Hall of Fame" is another winner. "When are you going to go fishing?" is a good question. After you've been able to discuss something of great significance like that, then tell him you quit your job. Timing is everything.

4. Don't command him.

Husbands have a way of going bonkers when they are told what to do. And, like it or not, they especially hate it when a woman demands something.

Men may have fragile egos. They might need to grow up. But these are the facts. Women usually need to lead men and not shove them. If you bark at a man and give him no choice, the outcome will not be pretty.

You can yell, "Fire, run for it!" and he might obey. But even then his first thought will probably be, "Says who?"

5. Be a friend.

How do you talk to your friends? Your husband is your ultimate friend and you need to talk to him in the same thoughtful way.

Have a million great conversations.

Is Your Bed Verdant?

One of the lovers in the Song of Solomon describes their bed as verdant (1:16). Since most beds are described as waterbeds, lumpy beds, or queen-sized beds, I had to scratch my head and ask: What in the world is a verdant bed?

Can you get a verdant bed on sale in the fall? Does it fold up in the daytime and become a sofa? Maybe it was a term used back then to describe a sleeping bag, though it's hard to imagine King Solomon and his wife snuggled up in a mummy bag.

So I looked up verdant, and the dictionary says it means "green." These two hot lovers had a green bed. Now I'm picturing a huge, four-poster bed with a green canopy. I imagine dark green pillowcases and a watermelon green bedspread.

But maybe I'm too practical. Maybe verdant doesn't refer to decorations. Possibly it refers not to the colors of the boudoir but rather to its bountiful richness and pleasure.

They thought of their bedroom as a garden filled with all manner of satisfying fruit and delicious produce. Their bedroom was in full bloom, pleasing to the eye, the smell, and to the touch.

Some people take the verse literally and believe the royal couple made love outside under the trees. We won't try to improve on that vision.

Don't get bogged down in the details of the picture. Most importantly, they looked at their bedroom as a place to enjoy the great, ripened fruit. With a sense of spontaneity, they could let go and roll around in the garden of love. (And the king without his crown!)

The word "boudoir" is French and has

its root in the word "pout." Sometimes it is a place to pout, but hopefully not often. More frequently it is a place to find physical fulfillment, to communicate love, and simply to enjoy.

May your bedroom be verdant. May it be a meadow, peaceful and serene. May it be a garden with variety and plenty. May it be the forest that fills up your senses. May it be a jungle where . . . maybe I'm getting carried away. You get the idea.

✦

Be Careful Who You Talk To

*H*ave you ever sat around in a gripe session discussing what's wrong with school? Before long everyone agrees that the dean is dumb, the teachers are uncaring, the tuition is too high, and the food tastes like pond scum. Who we talk to and listen to has a great effect on how we feel about something.

It wouldn't take long to find a half dozen people who are down on marriage. They are in marriages that aren't working, or their marriages are breaking up and they are understandably bitter. When someone's marriage is a miserable experience, it's hard for her to say much nice about it.

Be careful how much time you spend with friends who trash-talk marriage. If stores used that kind of advertising, they would soon close. Restaurants would go out of business; dog kennels would lose their poodles. It's difficult to maintain enthusiasm for something that is bad-mouthed week after week.

The people who don't like marriage are telling some truth. For some reason it isn't working for them. But the fact is that marriage is a terrific arrangement for millions of us. We relish the experience and thoroughly enjoy our companions. There are six or sixty good days for every disappointing one.

Surround yourself with people who are still in love. Ask happy couples what it takes to keep their relationship alive. Listen for hints on how to iron out a wrinkly marriage and make it smooth again.

The Bible tells us about keeping good company and walking with wise people

❖

(Proverbs 13:20). If we hang out with friends who mutter and murmur against marriage, the whole idea might begin to seem distasteful.

Find a happy person and say, "Tell me three things you like about marriage." Then find another and ask him the same thing. Before long you will have a sizable list of strong recommendations that will keep you in high spirits and thankful for the man in your life.

Carryover Burnout

The two of you have such a variety of interests. Music, camping, skiing, biking, school, friends, relatives, church, and a great deal more. Sometimes the temptation for multi-talented people is to become involved in so many interests that they have little energy left for each other.

Too many couples look back and say, "We just didn't have time for each other." And now they don't have each other.

Each of you has high expectations for yourself. You are good achievers, and neither of you likes to be idle. Those are terrific traits, especially if you don't forget to invest time and energy in each other.

Married couples of all ages often come home with no energy. They studied, they worked, they bowled, they listened to friends, and then they came home to crash. Now their relationship has to survive with whatever leftover energy they can conjure up.

Their marriage may not be ashes, but carryover burnout is killing their relationship. They gave their all at the office and there is not enough spark to keep the flame going at home.

When I hear about rich and famous people who are on their fifth marriage, I think, "What is the point?" Is a person really a success if she hasn't taken the time necessary to make the most important relationship in her life work?

All of us travel at different speeds. We can't all share the same priorities. But most people who reach their goals and sacrifice their marriages in the process wish they had put more energy into the relationship and made time together a priority.

❖

Three Nevers

There aren't many "nevers" in marriage. Who knows what tomorrow may bring and what you might want to do? But there are a few nevers. Some are obvious. Some are not.

Let me suggest three of the big ones.

1. Never diet.

Neither of you need to worry about this, but in case you think you do—don't. Dieting is a first-class happiness wrecker. Picture yourself half starving, head aching day and night, and an energy level two degrees lower than a slug.

With all of that going on, imagine yourself trying to maintain a vibrant relationship. Your odds are near zero.

I've been on all kinds of diets. I've eaten eggs until I clucked. Eaten grapefruit until my face shriveled. Nothing does more to derail a marriage than a spouse who has been eating pumpkin seeds for two days.

Eat less if you wish. Eat wisely if you choose. Exercise more if it fits. But never, never, never crash diet.

2. Never discuss old boyfriends and girlfriends.

It sounds cute enough. Why not mention an old steady and tease your partner for a bit? Most of us feel threatened by our spouse's memories of an old love. Even if it was nothing, we still tend to imagine it was a fiery torch.

We are too insecure to have the ghosts of past loves dragging chains through our bedrooms. If you want to tease, talk about his tennis swing, his new hat, or the way he butters his bread. Don't pull out his girlfriends or your boyfriends for entertainment value.

On a day when you least expect it, those

old stories have a way of being thrown back into your face.

3. Never tell a lie.

The temptation will be to tell a little lie so you can save your partner from pain. You might even rationalize and call it a "good lie." When we lie to someone who loves us, we put a crack in the glass shield known as trust. If we keep doing it, we eventually shatter that glass.

Often our partner has to handle real pain and hear the truth. He is old enough, mature enough, and strong enough to deal with disappointment and even heartache.

Once a spouse learns that his partner might lie, the relationship becomes shaky. It isn't worth it to lose trust merely to save your partner from pain.

  #

We Go Half Crazy

lamming doors and rattling pans can be heard at the most unexpected times. Everything seems to be going along well when suddenly your spouse starts to act like a bull beating on the gate of its pen. What in the world happened to your peaceful, playful partner? For the past fifteen minutes he has been snorting and puffing and grinding his teeth like he is about to blow up.

Without bogging down in a swamp of technical jargon, let's go directly to the simple explanation for ugly behavior. The fact is that sometimes we just go nuts. Does it have anything to do with body chemistry or background or temperament or too many demands? Maybe. But every once in a while without warning, without sense, without an evident cause, we go half crazy.

That's the human condition, and almost everyone suffers from it. Expect it. Expect it in your mate and expect it in yourself. If two people are going to live together, every now and then one of them is going to go bonkers.

Not that we hit each other or play knife tag around the kitchen table. That's serious stuff. But normal, average crazy is a malady that occasionally sweeps over all of us.

In order for life to run smoothly, we have to maintain a juggling act. We have six or eight balls to keep in the air at the same time. The balls are called psychological, spiritual, physical, vocational, relational, and what-have-you. We don't all juggle exactly the same balls.

Most of the time we juggle with a fair amount of precision. But now and again we accidently drop a ball or two. Rarely do we drop them all at once, but it can happen.

❖

When we start to drop the balls, we begin to go half crazy. Our behavior is irrational, our vocabulary is pointed and mean, our attitude hits foggy bottom. At that point we have entered the suburbs of Nutsville.

Fortunately we don't usually stay there long. One evening should about cover it. A couple of days is an overload. A person can only slam cabinet doors so many times before returning to rational behavior.

So be encouraged. The next time either of you jams dishes into the dishwasher, kicks the cat, or turns the CD up to double volume, say to yourself: someone's losing it. Then hunker down until crazy-time passes over.

❖

The Imperfect
Relationship

There are thousands of books and seminars available about marriage. Are marriages really falling apart in direct proportion to how many books, articles, videos, and classes are being taught?

It's a strange phenomenon.

Maybe marriage is being studied to death. We have begun to believe that marriage is a science, and all we need is the correct formula or series of formulas and we can make marriage work.

Certainly some information helps. Two

or three practical books might keep us on track. But marriage is not a science. We can't pour in two beakers of this, stir it with that, heat it to the proper temperature, and expect the right relationship to come out of the mix.

At best, marriage is an imperfect art, so we should expect an imperfect marriage. That doesn't mean we settle for a disastrous relationship. It doesn't mean we stop trying to improve what we have. But it does mean we need not drown in the sea of idealism.

I constantly meet couples who are embarrassed that their marriages have bumps and potholes. And invariably they are also afraid someone else will discover that their highway of happiness has its share of detours.

The normal, satisfying, prosperous relationship is the imperfect relationship. A perfect marriage would be an unbearable pain to maintain.

I hope you find that a relief. Inhale and exhale slowly. Can you feel the tension escaping from your body and putting your mind at ease?

If you accept the premise of the imperfect relationship, there won't be nearly as many crises. Hair in the sink, a towel on the floor, a harsh word or two won't be nearly as traumatic.

Eventually, you may even have to accept the shock that comes with imperfect children. Learning to love the imperfect partner is good training for when you become the imperfect parent.

In the final analysis, it's a fair deal. Since we are imperfect people, what else can we expect but imperfect relationships?

He Didn't Use
to Do That

*W*hen romance and reality collide, married partners moan this tune in a minor key. We groan that our spouse "didn't use to do that."

That doesn't mean we've been deceived and now have to face the real person. All of us know what happened. When two people go together, each of them puts his best foot forward. They celebrate their two-month anniversary of dating. He opens the car door, and he buys her candy. She eats the candy instead of complaining about her

118

diet (or she at least shares some with him).

After they get married, the two of them settle down and become more like themselves. That's the good news and the bad. We all need to become ourselves and take off our masks. My spouse needs to meet the real me. The tragedy is when one partner thinks he or she can stop being kind. If kindness is thrown out, misery flies in.

So—don't be surprised if your husband:

leaves his socks on the floor next to the hamper;

picks out his own movie on your "date night";

doesn't buy you a present for Valentine's Day;

has no idea how many years you've been married;

forgets to notice you've rearranged the furniture.

All this is natural. It's hard to live together and remember everything. Don't be shocked. Try not to be disappointed. It's tough to be thoughtful all of the time. You probably won't be either.

As you "settle in" together and become

more yourselves, you will see new forms of kindness develop. You will discover more adventures. Before long you will see character traits that will satisfy you even more than the gifts and pretenses you were used to.

You don't want to be single and date forever. It would be a shame to be engaged the rest of your life. Be thankful you have moved on to a better stage. Only in marriage will you get to meet the real person with all of his attributes and virtues.

He isn't the way he used to be. Enjoy getting to know who he really is.

Rules for Battle

We received some great gifts for our wedding. Nice people gave us silver trays and blankets and toasters. The gifts were all appreciated, but there was one thing I wish someone had given us. I wish someone had typed out a set of battle rules for marriage. We had no idea how to wage war. If couples are to battle and survive, they must engage each other in a civilized manner.

These are the rules we've learned the hard way over the years. Copy these and magnetize them to your fridge.

1. Stay in good shape.

If you get too tired, too hungry, or too lazy you won't be able to fight fair. Stay in training physically.

2. Avoid name calling.

"Listen, sewer breath" is hard to erase off the mental tape. (So are words like "chubby," "big ears," "airhead," and other colorful terms.)

3. Skip some rounds.

A sign of maturity is when you don't fight every time you hear the bell ring.

4. Never get physical.

Pushing, shoving, smacking, and grabbing are demeaning and threatening. They should never be a part of even the most intense battles.

5. Don't call relatives names.

Leave his unemployed brother, his deerpoaching cousin, and his moonshine-making uncle out of it. And never say, "You're just like . . ."

6. Don't be a wise guy.

When the battle heats up, don't try to insert a little caustic humor. This could get you a flying cup and saucer, a slammed door, or a locked bedroom. (These are just my guesses.)

7. Never be a comedian in bed.

What you think is funny about your partner's body, your partner may not think is funny.

8. Keep your battles short.

Always try to make up by bedtime. The Bible mentioned this before I did.

9. Don't pick a fight to make up.

Making up can be fantastic, but it's wrong to start a battle simply to improve your love life.

10. Never say "And another thing . . ."

Stick to the issue at hand. One battle at a time.

11. Don't get even.

Vengeance belongs to the Lord; so give it up.

12. Look for a conclusion.

Don't just agree to fight later. What are the two of you going to do about this?

Battling can be productive, but it has to be civilized.

Holidays and Vacations

*G*etting together with family is great fun. But some families dread special occasions because they turn into wars. Before the day is over a relative makes a rude observation. Someone else chimes in, "What do you mean by that?" Suddenly one or two say they won't attend any more family celebrations.

The best way to have family get-togethers is to hang loose and keep your sense of humor. Because we love each other and continue to communicate, someone is bound to make a few dumb remarks. We probably have already. Overlook them.

124

❖

Love and relationships can't survive without a healthy dose of patience, forgiveness, and forgetfulness. Maybe that's why the Lord taught us so much about it—He knew we were going to have relatives.

Forgive me if I express my opinion of your choice of wallpaper in the living room. Sometimes I lack tact. Cut me some slack if I fail to notice your new hairstyle; I almost never notice such things. And if I suggest your politics are pitiful, that's just the way I am. Try to love me anyway. I'm a relative.

None of us is obligated to attend a family gathering. Christmas doesn't have to be at our place and it doesn't have to be December 25. Neither your mother nor I will perish if Thanksgiving isn't like it used to be. If you skip Thanksgiving, we'll have you over for Groundhog Day.

Occasions are special and we love them. But we know that times change and so do practices. We enjoy our little traditions but we will also enjoy new ones.

When I ask my friends what they are doing for the holidays, they almost always answer in terms of people. A son is coming on Tuesday; a daughter and her family are driving in on Wednesday. They don't answer in terms of pies, presents, or duck hunting. They talk about the people they love.

If get-togethers change, we can handle that. We simply don't want them to stop. We can meet in our living room or yours. We can sit by a stream or climb a mountain together. Whether it's talking, eating, traveling, playing, snoozing, walking, or working puzzles. As long as we're together.

❖

Do's About Sex

The big word in sex is "do." I've never seen a couple suffer mental damage from too much sex. If sex is taken care of correctly, it adds greatly to the quality of life and to the strength of the relationship. In other words, go for it and keep going for it.

If you need help with technique or technical questions, get a good book about sex and read it together. Meanwhile consider a few positive guidelines.

1. Do what you want.

The Bible says the marriage bed is undefiled. In other words, it's a terrific recreational device that should not be ignored.

The only way we wreck married sex is by being unfaithful. How you do it, when you do it, or how often you do it isn't anyone else's business.

It's good to abstain for spiritual pursuits, job interviews, and trips to the laundromat. Otherwise your sex life belongs to you.

2. Keep it a priority.

Working two or three jobs and going to school doesn't leave a lot of free time. My suggestion is you drop the aerobics class and make love. The first few years you can get more exercise in the bedroom anyway.

Don't try to do everything and be everywhere. Keep lovemaking high on the list next to prayer and food. Leave the dishes, don't wash windows, and if necessary, don't dust for two years. A dusty living room may be a sign of a good sex life (I'll check your coffee table next time I visit)!

3. Begin early.

Save your best energy for lovemaking. You can droop around and be dreary while you vacuum. Sex deserves your extra effort. You can always take a nap the next day at

✦

lunchtime (preferably together) to make up for lost sleep.

4. Take sex vacations.

A change of scenery is one sure way to keep your love life vibrant. Your home can become a place that calls out for work. It reminds you of chores to do, bills to be paid, and clothes to be ironed.

When you get a few extra bucks, take off for a motel. If you stop too close to home, you might get a funny look from the clerk, but who cares? Ask him if there is a special love rate.

5. Use sex to communicate.

Sex says, "I love doing it with you. I love being with you, and you really make me happy." Sex makes each of you feel special and wanted. Its number one role in marriage is to say "I love you" with words and with your bodies. That's living.

Counting Candy Bars

When we go on a trip together, your mother keeps a record of every dime we spend. I can't tell you how often I have bought a candy bar or a pack of mints only to have Pat stand by my side and write down the amount. It used to embarrass me.

Now I simply accept your mother's habit and I've learned to appreciate its value. Pat always knows where the money comes from and where it's going. She doesn't care how I spend our money but she wants it accounted for. And she wants to know what expenses are coming up. If our trip to Kansas City cost $257.13, she insists on knowing exactly that.

Our life hasn't always been so regimented. I used to throw money around with little idea of where it was going. When I bought our first Mazda, I didn't realize we still owed money on our other vehicle. That's how you go broke and drive your spouse insane.

I've always hated the word "budget." Budget sounds boring, restrictive, and painful. But in reality, if budgets help you keep your finances in control, they are liberating and exciting.

There are many formulas for family budgets and most of them probably work. The simplest place to start is this: take a piece of paper. Draw a line down the middle. At the top of one side write "income." Above the other column write "expenses." Then make a habit of recording your transactions.

A hundred dollars comes in. Sixty dollars is spent on groceries. Two hundred dollars is earned. Three hundred dollars goes for rent. That's the way it works. You keep an eye on what is going out and what is coming in. What payments are coming up? Adjustments may have to be made. Some couples adjust, while others mess up and are terribly sorry.

Maybe you don't need to count candy bars. But there needs to be a system of control. If money is out of control, it's like a hillside without terraces or ground cover. When it rains, the mud gets washed away before anyone realizes what is happening.

If you start a budget early, you are far ahead of many couples. Too many wait until the first disaster hits. They get an ugly letter from the utility company or a credit card company or the bank. Only then do they admit financial chaos.

Get a piece of paper. Draw a line. How much did you spend on yogurt this afternoon?

Simply Shocked

The old cliche about marrying a stranger is basically true. Despite our best attempts to sound the depths and check the mettle of our lover, there is much we will never know until we have been married for some time. Only then can we find new treasures in our spouse. It also takes a while to unearth parts of the dark side.

All of us have a dark side. It may not be large and it may not show up often, but it's there nevertheless. We all have an evil nature and even if we try hard to suppress it, the gruesome character eventually pushes itself through.

❖

Don't be shocked. Our prejudices, our intolerance, our self-doubts, our temper, our insecurities, our unreasonableness can be held down only so long. There is no ultimate intimacy unless we allow our dark side to surface and expose all of who we are.

Don't be too shocked that your partner sometimes has the uglies. All of us do. I expect my spouse to be understanding about my shortcomings. It is only fair that I allow room for her sins, too.

Those who go pearl diving frequently find more than little white jewels. Sometimes they are confronted with dangerous creatures who live to destroy. Pearl divers take risks because they know the prize is worth the effort.

Intimacy is never risk free. There is no way to reveal my good side without eventually exposing my mean side, too. Out of fear of being rejected for showing their ugly sides, many couples remain married for twenty years without reaching a high degree of intimacy. Their lives are spent with the lid tightly sealed for fear of what might escape.

✧

With time and love the monsters might become less in number. Those fearsome creatures might raise their gruesome heads less often. But they are there.

The best answer is never to keep the lid shut. We will miss too many good virtues. Just don't get knocked out of your chair when the creature feature starts to play. All of us have monsters.

❖

Kindling for Dreams

One of the things I especially appreciate about God is His willingness to promote dreams. Our happiness isn't God's primary concern, but it does make His top ten list.

The fulfillment of your mate's dreams should be on your top ten list, too. Maybe not number one or even number two, but his dreams should show up near the top.

If Phil wants to study the purple butterflies of Nova Scotia, you could begin collecting maps of eastern Canada. If you want to go spelunking in upper Idaho, he could start gathering flashlights.

Dream pushers make great spouses. When their partners begin striking matches, they go out looking for wood to add to the flame.

Some partners take on the role of the dream dowser. They think their job is to stop their mates from drifting off on wild goose chases. When they accept that role, they become like gigantic dark clouds and their partners will soon learn to resent them.

We can't always share our partner's dreams. We might even think the dreams are dumb or crazy. But we must defend their right to dream. And sometimes we have to carry kindling to help them build fires.

It's sad to see relationships where one partner dreams and the other simply nods approval. The nodder stands off and watches the dreamer pursue his or her goal. It's painful for the dreamer if the spouse never helps carry kindling for his dreams.

At the local county fair I always admire the husbands who are there to carry in the boxes of crafts for their wives. When I go to a church league softball game I notice the wife who is keeping score—or playing right field. Even at chess tournaments I see a spouse or two silently cheering for their mates.

Of course, it would be a shame if we spent our entire lives carrying kindling for someone else. Each of us has to find a lark and chase it. And when we catch one, hopefully our spouse will be running at our heels carrying an extra net.

When loving acts are named one by one, the act of carrying kindling is a big one. It is a work of selflessness. A work of sacrifice. Even a work of God.

The Blame Game

It's early Monday morning. You reach into the fridge for the milk and, lo and behold, there isn't any. Now whose fault is that? Who drank all the milk? Did your husband know the milk was used up on Sunday but was too lazy go to the store? Exactly who sabotaged this morning's modest breakfast plans?

That's the way many couples deal with problems. Instead of looking for solutions to problems, they are busy trying to assign blame. Sometimes we spend a lot of energy trying to build secure walls around ourselves so we don't have to take the blame or be responsible for our actions.

Marriage always fares poorly in the blame game. Assigning blame is an act of wounding one's partner. Probably most of us would rather have our spouses wounded instead of ourselves.

We shift the issue. Instead of solving our real problem (the empty milk bottle), we create a second problem (a guilty spouse).

Blame is a hot potato. You toss it to your mate and just as quickly your mate throws it back in your direction. You have now entered the great milk bottle debate. You level accusations. You make charges. You raise defenses. You bring up countercharges. You reintroduce questions about the empty jelly jar. Soon you rehash last month's incident about the butter left by the sink.

By now the skirmish over milk has widened into full-fledged war. Before long, name-calling and snide remarks enter the battle. Combatants turn their heels to each other and march off in an indignant huff.

Despite all of the posturing, poking, and pleas of self-righteousness, the problem of the empty bottle goes unresolved. The real issue should have been "How in the world can we see to it that there is milk in the fridge next time we need it?" Instead, you create hurt feelings and raise hostilities that never should have seen the light of day.

We all have conflicts. That's the price we pay for living with each other. A small price at that. Smart couples look for ways to resolve conflicts instead of ways to cast blame.

The real issue was the missing milk at breakfast. We need to keep it that simple.

Cream-Filled Shoes

*L*ighten up! Chill out! Simmer down! Or whatever the term is for people who need a sense of humor. Couples who learn to laugh at themselves in a good-natured way are almost always the happiest.

Humor doesn't mean we learn to make fun of our spouses. It means we have instead mastered the skill of occasionally laughing at ourselves.

Couples often flounder because they are uptight, defensive, and insecure. They take themselves far too seriously. Sensitive to every spoken word, they live on the edge, afraid of the next remark that could be construed as an insult.

Give it a rest. Don't degrade yourself, but look at the lighter side of your appearance and personality.

Under my right eyebrow I have a wart. I've learned to appreciate my wart and almost treat it like a friend. If it wasn't for my wart, I would look just about perfect. I don't think I could stand the pressure of looking just about perfect. That's also why I wear glasses, comb my hair so it looks thicker, and maintain a slightly double chin. Otherwise my fine looks could get me in trouble.

Why not be proud of our differences? Why do we need to look like the people on television commercials?

Learn to laugh a little on a bad hair day. That's maturity. Laugh a little at your eccentric parents. Look for humor in your relationship. Don't be afraid to make fun of your own cooking once in a while. Not every recipe is worth defending.

Humor doesn't have to be demeaning. Don't use it to attack each other. But the couple that stops laughing together stops playing together and, before long, will stop loving together.

If we take ourselves too seriously, we will probably take our marriage too seriously. If we take our marriage too seriously, it becomes harsh and brittle.

Sometime when you think your marriage has become too dull, fill up Phil's shoe with shaving cream. I can't predict what will happen, but it won't be dull.

A Time to Whisper

As you may have noticed, the members of our household have never been good shouters. We have done a little shouting, but we have never become skilled at it.

While I admit to our inability to shout well, let me say a few words in defense of whispering. A soft-spoken word under control is a rare jewel that needs to be presented more often.

Some marriages are packed with people yelling, calling names, and screaming. Somewhere people have gotten the notion that loud arguing is healthy for a relationship. Some couples feel something is wrong if they are not regularly shouting at their mates. As if yelling were the magic key to effective communication.

Be careful that you never make it a practice to shout at Phil. When a conversation hits a screaming pitch, there are few other places it can go. If yelling can no longer escalate, a couple usually turns to physical forms of expression. People tend to hit and hurt when words no longer serve them well.

Convinced that they cannot win their argument with steel-like logic, they resort to pushing, shoving, and throwing objects.

It's important that we say the words that need to be said. A little volume might help for emphasis, but too much volume detracts from the message.

Whispering is a great attention grabber. Have you ever tried to outshout a group of children or teens? If they are too noisy, whispering often calms them down. Yell, and they will try to outyell you.

Whispering is soft. Whispering is soothing. Whispering helps a couple focus.

Whispering isn't threatening or frightening. Whispering is disarming. Whispering says you are under control but you have something in mind that needs to be communicated.

Pillow-talk at its best is whispering, never shouting. Love and mushy-goo talk should be barely audible. An invitation to go to bed early should usually be spoken softly and breathed directly into the ear.

Corrective and confrontational conversation can also be communicated in measured tones with direct, frank, and honest words, without theatrics.

I like the verse that tells us God "stilled the storm to a whisper" (Psalm 107:29). Storms make people head for cover and defend themselves. Whispers are intriguing conversations filled with potential.

Marriage Lite

*L*ite pancake syrup is a terrific idea. It seems to have the same good taste with only about a third of the calories. Lite mayonnaise, lite peaches, lite whipped cream. All are a little less, cut back a tad, for healthier eating.

But the slimmer, trimmer, thinner marriage isn't nearly healthy enough.

Marriage is worth the extra effort and sacrifice it will take to keep your commitment firm and your compassion flowing.

Too many couples cut back on their marriages. They have found a carload of other things to do. A husband once told me,

❖

"We seem to get along a lot better when we don't see each other."

No doubt some people overdose on marriage. Too much togetherness is dangerous. Called smothering, it bugs most of us sometimes. But the solution to smothering isn't marriage lite. The solution is relationship balance.

Don't be fooled by the "We get along better apart" crowd. It doesn't have to be that way. Marriage that is too lite has a way of running out of energy.

Never apologize for working hard and investing in your marriage to keep it up to full strength.

✦

Will You Ever Wonder?

I asked them to close their eyes and bow their heads. They were a great group of young married couples that I had learned to know over the years. Then I asked the big question. "Would you raise one finger if you have ever wondered whether you married the right person?" Half the group raised one finger.

That didn't surprise me. I thought the percentage would have been more than that.

Wondering is, after all, merely a mental exercise. I've been to Tibet many times, but only in my mind. It's effortless and inex-

❖

pensive. Mental journeys don't take much work.

Don't be shocked if someday into your mind pops the ugly question: "Did I marry the right person?"

The answer to the question isn't found by looking back at your wedding day. That is history. The answer is found in today. The only question that matters is: "Am I now married to the right person?" And the answer is still yes. Time and effort may be needed for you to see the potential for your relationship to grow in love and respect again. But as you commit yourselves to sorting out the differences that brought on the doubts, your marriage will be as genuine, viable, and hopeful as you saw it to be from the beginning.

The day may come for each of you when you ask yourself if this was the right choice. Don't be frightened by the question. Too many feel the very question itself is an admission of defeat.

Let it come and let it go. What you should or should not have done doesn't matter. The real challenge is "What will you do now?"

Almost all marriages are real, viable, and hopeful. Love, and work with what you have.

❖

If We Had it
to Do Over

W e don't want to do it over. Our
marriage is too satisfying to ever
want to start another one. We can't say if it's
a good marriage because we don't know
what the standard is.

All I know is that God has been faithful,
and I can hardly wait to come home after
work each night. If I could pick one person
to walk on a beach with, one person to sit
by the fireplace with, one person to hug and
cry with, the answer always comes up Pat.

I refuse to have regrets—simply because I think it's the wrong way to look at life. But as I reflect, there are a couple of hundred things I might do better if I could start the clock over. Maybe some of these will prove helpful to you.

I'd concentrate more on giving love and less on taking it.

I'd say "no" more to others and less to my wife.

I'd accept myself more and stop depending on her for my self-worth.

I'd date my wife once a week even if it's just for coffee.

I'd call home more because I still get a kick out of hearing her voice on the phone.

I'd rub that spot where she likes to be rubbed.

I would praise her for who she is and never again try to mold her into someone else.

I'd thank God more often for the gift He allowed me to keep.

I'd listen a little more to her kind of music.

I'd stay in bed longer after making love and hold her.

154

❖

I'd buy her more peppermints and gingersnap cookies because they're her favorites.

I'd get angry a lot less and work on patience.

I'd forgive her every time, and I'd do it right away.

The list is getting long and I'm getting mushy. I hope it's a help. We don't have many years here, and it's a total rush to think that God let me have a wife who fills my heart with love. What a deal.

❖

Promises From Me

Wherever you live and whatever you do, I want to keep my relationship with you. Through time and distance this could be increasingly difficult. I understand that. But I am willing to make the adjustments necessary to keep in touch and stay close.

With that in mind I want to make some promises. I've asked the Lord to help me keep them.

• I promise to give advice.

But only when I'm asked and then very sparingly. Adults don't need a popcorn pop who is always telling them what to do.

❖

- I promise to be happy.

I won't try to hold on to you by com-plaining and searching for sympathy. God is extremely good to us. Some are tempted to manipulate their children by whining. For-get that. I owe you my own happiness.

- I promise to respect you.

Your world and mine are not the same. I will try not to put your interests down or treat your tastes as trivial. You both are bright, creative, and adventuresome. Those traits are to be honored.

- I promise to listen.

It's the golden gift. Listening is an act of love. When you want to talk, I promise you attention, energy, involvement, pa-tience, care, and every encouragement. I want to be a person who can share your dreams, aspirations, fears, disappoint-ments, and joys.

- I promise not to pry.

When the two of you aren't getting along, I won't be Mr. Fixit. I'll let you two work it out. Your mutual solutions are the ones that will last. A little advice if I'm

✧

asked, like I said, but I promise not to interfere.

- I promise to be myself.

I'll sing when I do dishes, bore you about old movies, and beat you mercilessly at Nerts if you dare play. I won't burden you by becoming the perfect parent and father-in-law. I probably could do it, but I refuse. Except for a few refinements, I'll stay what I've always been. Me.

- I promise to be equal.

No more "because I said so" or "don't argue with me, little lady." We've been on a level playing field too long to ever go back to "Daddy says" again.

- I promise never to forget.

Never to forget the curly hair and dimples, the Sunday in the hospital, the daddy/daughter date night, or the doughnut shops. I also won't forget what a wonderful woman you have become.

Books for Adults by William Coleman

Before I Give You Away
Eight Things Not to Say to Your Teen
It's Been a Good Year
Knit Together
Measured Pace
Newlywed Book
*Ten Things Your Teens Will Thank
    You For . . . Someday*
*Today's Handbook of Bible Times and
    Customs*
What Makes Your Teen Tick?